The Marriage of Space and Time

The Marriage of Space and Time

Jed Myers

MoonPath Press

Poetry
ISBN 978-1-936657-42-1

Cover photo © Rosanne Olson website: rosanneolson.com

Author photos by Alina Rios

Design: Tonya Namura
using Gill Sans (display) and Minion Pro (text)

MoonPath Press is dedicated to publishing the finest poets
of the U.S. Pacific Northwest.

MoonPath Press
PO Box 445
Tillamook, OR 97141

MoonPathPress@gmail.com

http://MoonPathPress.com

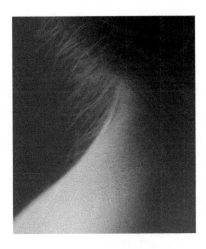

To my mother and father,
Phyllis and Jerry Myers,
in loving memory.

They faithfully engaged me in the art of finding the words.

Acknowledgments

With my ongoing thanks, I acknowledge here the publications where the following poems in this collection first appeared.

"Close to Home"—*Bracken*

"First Farewell"—*Poetry Northwest*

"Morning Rush"—*Zócalo Public Square*

"Asylum"—*Cultural Weekly*

"The Truth Takes Lunch"—*The Southeast Review*

"These Arias"—*Broad River Review*

"Between Reykjavik and Glasgow"—*Magma*

"Note"—*Chróma*

"Before Going In"—*The Briar Cliff Review*

"Goodnight Rhyme"—*Corium Magazine*

"So We Spoke"—*Slippery Elm*

"Not White"—*Clackamas Literary Review*

"This Disappearing"—*LiTFUSE Anthology*

"Yahrzeit"—*Harpur Palate*

"After Parking at Starbucks"—*Cultural Weekly*

"Two Men Saying Goodbye"—*Hospital Drive*

"Shadow-Ink"—*Cloudbank*

"Seasonal"—*The Adirondack Review*

"Birds Over a Marsh"—*Strokestown International Prize Shortlist*

"The Impossible"—*New Southerner*

"The Temperature"—*Common Ground Review*

"My Brother's Own Throat"—*Oxford Magazine*

"Love Poem Written in Broad Darkness"—*Pretty Owl Poetry*

"Here After"—*Cultural Weekly*

"The Rose"—*The Midwest Quarterly*

"Geometry of the Orbits"—*The Greensboro Review*

"Pull of the Moon"—*Valparaiso Poetry Review*

"I'll See Her Turning"—*Crosswinds Poetry Journal*

"Signature"—*Prime Number Magazine*

"Catch"—*New Southerner*

"In the Shade by the Water"—*Slippery Elm*

"I Know You from Somewhere"—*New Southerner*

"Love's Home"—*Broad River Review*

"Night on the Way Back from the Metolius River"—
Cider Press Review

"No Other"—*Dark's Channels* (chapbook, *Iron Horse
Literary Review*)

"What I Did"—*The Summerset Review*

***

"Asylum" also appeared in *Portside*. "The Temperature" also
appeared in *Serving House Journal*. "The Truth Takes Lunch"
also appeared in the chapbook *Dark's Channels* (*Iron Horse
Literary Review*). "Pull of the Moon" also appeared in the
anthology *for Love of Orcas* (Wondering Aengus Press).

Gratitude

I am moved to express my thanks to many, allies, friends, family, mentors, all of whom are present in this gathering of poems. I cannot name all these dear souls, but I can say here that without the faith and support of Alina Rios, Jonas Myers, Isaac Myers, Lily Myers, Ford Myers, Charlene Breedlove, Lana Hechtman Ayers, Seth Cohen, Peter Munro, Ted McMahon, Ashley Brumett, Philip Randolph, Caleb Thompson, Erika Michael, Rosanne Olson, Lyn Coffin, Bart Baxter, Jim Bertolino, Anita Boyle, Chris Jarmick, John Burgess, Thomas Hubbard, and a good few who've been part of NorthEndForum and Easy Speak, I might never have gathered these poems at all.

My thanks goes also, in memoriam, to the physicist Jack Tessman, my teacher at Tufts long ago, who helped me see more deeply into the poetic symmetries of the cosmos.

JM

Table of Contents

Union

The Marriage of Space and Time

Space

Present Company

Wait now—I ask this
of myself, alone, in bed,
not turning the light off yet—

the meeting's not over. Listen,
I implore myself in the quiet,
and with my quiet address the ceaseless

exhalation of the basement furnace
up through the vent. Or do I detect
the socks' congress, dresser's top drawer?

Same range as pigeon-flock lift-off,
jet coming in from the north, some wind,
noise in the circuit between eardrums

and brain. Are you there? I venture
the question, and watch the twin swirls
in the dresser's symmetric veneer—

Look, say those eyes under
the stern brows of the brass pulls,
now that you wonder, feel the moon lean

your lymph toward the Pacific? Gaia
keeps the quilt to your chest,
your heart and the whole of you close

to her life-beating death-eating breast.
You're right, I hear in the air
with no hope of nailing the source,

your Grandmother's dybbuks have dissolved
not into nothing—into the strings
between eternally entangled things,

so, sleep, dream, as you know
the meeting is never over. Enter
the dark with us, animal.

Close to Home

I follow someone into the trees,
out of the light, as if to reenter
a dream, but this bramble's thorned

for real. I'm not onto a trail
but a visual ripple, a rustle, snap
of a twig. Back of my hand

fresh-streaked red. I can't say
I know these woods, haven't been
that attentive. But someone feels his way

into the shade ahead—a mud-fellow,
forager, original nomad
hid in the cowl of our civil distraction,

invisible. Unless we consider
that flash just now in the laurel
more than a gust, not a squirrel

starting up a dark branch
after a few breaths' vigilance, not
a sparrow jostling the long leaves

as it lifts toward its nest, but someone
who regards me as a guest,
and who will show me—close to home

in this strip of forest bounded by streets—
a clutch of chanterelles, straw-gold in moss
at a fir's feet, where I've stumbled

soon enough, trusting a ghost.

First Farewell
—for my mother

Now I'll whisper to you from here.
You're out of that thinned envelope
on its brittle frame. Now

I'll say what I will—you'll find it
clear, your wonder no longer limited
by the late neuronal fray. Now

you may entertain some questions
the pull of the earth, hunger, and hurt
insisted you tuck away. Now

I'll see you risen, my heart's eye
open. It's you in the leaf-shimmer
I'm walking under. Now

it's you in the vapor nestled
in the ravine as I take the footbridge
toward the pub around dusk. Now

you'll take what forms you will
to explore—your translucent plumage
silver before the moon now.

I'll listen for what you whisper—
what you, no longer daughter, wife,
or mother, discover. What is love now?

Morning Rush

Now we're fissioned—it releases
enough desire to fuel the empire.
That's my smudged vision on this

frost-fogged, steamed street
at night's end in these bright overhead
cones and sweeping twin beams.

We are a flood of particles
stripped from our kin clusters,
spilled bridge elevator tunnel,

sluiced river of want, huffing
to fill our slots and seats, each
thriver promised the dollars

good for what? Pacifiers
to soothe our atomized selves—good
for ales or amaros, sliders or oysters,

smokes blades benzos syringes,
needles made to pierce or to paint,
private conquest games thumb-click

joystick semiautomatic, videoed
nakedness draped in latex to lace—
we're held in the charged field

predawn till after dusk, grinning
through gritted teeth. Seems a choice
to each, fingers a blur at the keys,

eyes tracking the customer's,
long as we're granted our own
intelligent phone and it lights

to our touch, our aloneness isn't
bottomless, and we have our series
to stream, whose company sings

in our catacombs. It occurs to me
that the empire is alive inside
our anatomy. We're subdivided,

as an old house turned apartments—
the abstinent grouch upstairs
who stomps and pounds *Shut up!,*

and the hedonic wrestlers below
who don't care if the jerk can't sleep
and must rise in the dark to shoot

through the tube to work. And what
do I note, or invent, in the straight
faces cresting the exit steps?

They press past on the sidewalk,
thin air partitions between.
We're paved apart from the dirt

and clothed in tones we paint cars
and kitchens, kept driven without
crosstalk or recognition, and swept

in this diurnal rhythm, task
to permitted intermission and back.
It's a hard vision. Then again

some of us winter well, suspended
in this separateness—I saw you
surface close to mercurial dawn,

into a school of coats, in a rose
flush of exertion. It was eons
ago, yesterday. Do you know

how dangerous it's become to loiter
at subway exits? I've got to
have my brain on the 39th floor,

at the monitor in five minutes.
And if before I turn I see you,
one of the human ions in the flux

up from the underground, then?
That might be all the enmeshment
we get. A trace of heart's witness

off like a note corked in a flask
across the turbulence. I wouldn't
dive through the flood to face you.

But I want you to know you were seen—
the blood in your cheeks, a defiant
innocence I'll daydream I saw

in the soft set of your lips, the unspent
reserve of your love I was sure of
without one spark of evidence.

Asylum

I'll offer you passage toward asylum
through the canals of my ears—please come
now, straight from the radio station.
I don't know who you'll find here
who speaks your language. But already
my grandmother calls to you in her Yiddish
as she chops beets for our borscht.

Your face, gritty in front page ink—
I think you could hide if you had to
in any odd shadow. But quick—
under these mom-and-pop storefront awnings
my eyelids. Please, come back
behind the shop, where we live—yes,
the kitchen. The future ferments

here in our memories' brine. We've pressed
fine slices of reddened smoked fish,
gift of the parted seas, upon bread
fresh-risen on the yeasts of the West.
And let us eat by the candles we've dipped
in the wax of our histories' hives, our stories
a weave, the wool of our sheep

on our shoulders. Too many have died—
there are all kinds of sudden fire,
and all the sparks one fear—the other comes
seeking asylum, what we've secured
only a few breaths before, and what
shall we offer? Here, my grandfather's chair,
and the shawl he brought across the water.

The Truth Takes Lunch

I'm the tide rising higher, acidified
shoals, young oyster shells decomposed.

And the odd legions of rain last week
off the sea that settled your dust,

and, yes, mine are the clear-cuts'
mudslides. I'm the buried road.

Try to keep me in line. I twist
like a river. I don't follow your signs.

I'm old as the asteroids' ice
in your blood. Young as a thought. I quote

Noah's dove—out over the flood
between these edifices, a leaf,

or is it a shred of document tossed
aloft on the turbulence, it flickers

chaotically toward you, and you take it
as meant. A message I've sent. Well,

I do watch the poles melt. I wash
the drowned white bear's bones. I swallow

the earth-burners' plumes, and blow
the ten million prisoners' whispers through

the trees where you take your lunch. Listen—
I give you the gunman's leer

like another leaf, this one in the pond
of the lens of the dead man's camera.

I am that membranous small egg of space
that holds the fallen apple's seed

through the season of rot. And I'm the lace
of interstices in the soil—I sip

the brook's trickle into the dark
to the roots of the lost man's shade. I am

your thirst for one more gust off the river
before your device warns you you must

get to the elevator and press
on in your service. I'm your delay,

the extra seconds your eye's on the blaze
the sun makes of the surface, the water

a starry display. The toddler's face,
her chin milk-wet on a sleeveless shoulder.

And I'm the blades of afternoon light
that will slice the air of the hearing chamber.

Silent gavel out of the sky
like a meteor, I'll rupture the idol

the lie in a register you can't hear.
I'm the spring in the breast of the mountain

you'll climb through the mud and gravel
to gather and sing, to drink

my cold clear mineral question
out of the core of the world. It could be

quick as a screech of brakes, or soon
as you step off on the wrong floor.

These Arias

It swells and breaks through the beeps
in the packed checkout zone after work,

spills from a crosswalk's crowd of heads,
echoes off window glass on the bus,

and, at the bar now, I'm awash in this
harsh talk-music. Hurt's waters gush

and flood, collapse down unparted onto us
far from any far shore. I say we are

born for such drowning. *Then he actually,
how could she, can you believe....*

No one's making it anywhere near
the manna. We manage a nostril

or two in the air. The crash comes
cold and familiar, old shock we know—

oh, we see it coming. Another
Manhattan? *All men are, aren't all women....*

It's louder here than the tall surf slapping
the cliffs at Cape Flattery. The plaint surges

wherever we congregate. There aren't measures
to fence these notes. And we can't cork

this roar—it starts after all as the earth's own
cry. A dark-matter moon of love's

urgency draws the wound-fluid
up through our cores. Listen—can't hear

Pandora's speaker cones pumping what is it
Madonna or Macklemore into the churn?

Neither can I, though the bass shivers
the populous mirror behind the bar. This live

choral turmoil, tide of tossed wishes,
collides with itself all about us, thunder

enough to muffle the digital schlock.
Look—our tongues stir a spume thick

as the head on that quick-spigotted Guinness
just slid past in the slosh. *Why*

did he hide it, she tried to wreck my life,
he isn't worth it, it blasts. But who,

if anyone, gets it? Fitful ritual
din of lament—mouthfuls pour from us

only to swirl away down the great storm drain
out of the present forever. There

in the glow of the liquor shelves' rows,
stoppered and screwcapped red gold and clear

comforts, the hipster at work drops
a splash of amaro to blood-tinge my bourbon,

tests it himself with a fingertipped straw,
and, as his eyebrows rise, I'm encouraged—

I'll ride a stretch of ease even while
the chop's this wild. Listen. All of these

lonely arias aloft and caroming
off the walls—*he never told me,*

I knew she would—a consonance, one sea's
constant harmonics, one dream's song.

Dirge for Wanderers

Today again, in the market, never
mind what I came for, that glare
on the stainless containers, offerings

lit to wet gleam by a fluorescent
flicker shaking the nerves, rhythmic
whine of the deli section's slicing

machines, the turbulent slosh
and chop of impatient shoppers'
voices, clop of heels on hard tile,

jingly scrape of some soft-rock oldie
meant to soothe and appeal, storewide
overhead jeer of deal-of-the-day

announcements—it happened, I reeled
inside, between hot soups and seafood,
receded into an aura only I

saw, I playing the nucleus
in my own bluish electron cloud,
I a great and uncertain distance

removed. Have you ever found yourself
peering out of the sudden recess
your overwhelm's drilled? Hard downshift

out of second nature to first,
pull of a separate gravity, some other
sort of particle—I stood there

and lost all scale. The field of me
swallowed the world, and the whole planet
grew utterly small, one of the countless

spores whirling about in the radiance
currents. Well, I'd only recoiled,
collapsed back into that lair

where Superman and The Flash once were
my nurturers, where I saw Einstein
get his hair frizzed, where gulls gliding

over the Delaware River taught a kid
effortlessness, the summer Atlantic's
breakers tumbled me till I emerged

through the froth to suck air
again, learning I'd live. A few moments
that far under the surface, number

and time twisted, I am billions
in one, ancient and young, the future
earth a char-crusted roast and still

a hot swirl of dust yet to congeal
into a sphere of itself. Before my birth
and after all these limbed forms

burn and disperse, in this deep refuge
where no one noticed I'd perched,
there's no such thing as aloneness.

I heard the meat-cutter's cough, cold
waterfall down the cavern's dark walls
a rumbling dirge for wanderers. All

in a matter of seconds I'd plummeted
into a private pool, a fusion
below the layers of our lonely roles,

and just as soon I was risen
into the irritant dazzle of clear plastic
tight on the flesh of the world.

Our Empty Palaces

Look with me at the upside-down city,
air castles whose squared-off spires butt
into the ground—negative
of our density, all breath, this empire
fills with the lights that enter its halls
off its stone and glass walls and up
yes up from the sky. We crawl its ceilings
like insects.

        Now you see it
a moment, but lose it again like that
chalice between the profiles. Doesn't it
keep us convinced, this gravity? As it is
psyche inverts the retina's image
each instant to set the world right
so to speak. I think we live
heads dangling toward the source,

the sea of sky, the before, beneath,
and at night, let's say we look deep
into the generous fires that made us.
To fly to the stars is to leap
loose and plummet back to that seafloor
whose immense jets of froth gave us loft,
sent us high to fashion our hives
on these suspended crusts,

           these earths,
where the thrust that launched us presses us
yet to street, sidewalk, grass,
and I want us to feel how we're stuck
here at the tops of our empty palaces.

Making the best of it are we? Blasting
holes in the dirt we never burst through
to the pure dark heights, do we Love?

After the Master Class

The urban word artist's trained himself
to cast the spooled web of his hurts
from his chest, invisible breath-pulsed

spell through his mouth onto the next
school of hearts, without getting caught
in his own net or anyone's yet.

Scalp shaved (where the crop was snipped
to a bristle, had been a thick thatch…)
for his new look on the workshop circuit,

he knows without thought how to pitch it
posed for the world mirror lens. He delivers
a surged lineated prose with his eyes wide

open like soul's windows on distances
over his listeners' heads. His lines,
like gravity waves, curve the surrounding

contours, bending desires his way
through the supple bodies of the gathered
undergrads, MFA holders and hopefuls,

one of whom tonight orbits close
in the dark hotel bar. She's old enough,
nothing out of bounds here. He offers

to look over what she wanted to show him
before, this time in his room with some
fine sipping rum. She may remember

a night she meandered off the earthbound
world-line of her life, or she might
suffer a rhythm of spasms, a shame

and its rage in the visceral crucible
where her words remain caged, never
loosed after all to the word artist's pull.

Between Reykjavik and Glasgow

We are poor indeed if we are only sane.
                    —D.W. Winnicott

Sometimes I hear the choruses—
most often on a plane. The engines'
screaming away out under the wings

opens the inner registers. You know,
hours unable to sleep in the air,
head's topple wakes you just as you doze—

a primed neural net finds music
in ceaseless noise. My eyes are closed
now in 10C, bright North Atlantic

morning light through my lids while we're out
over the clouds, and uninvited
it enters, via the whirr of the turbines,

here from wherever, a chanting
in strata, those uncountable voices—
deepest of earnest bassos and up

the layers, ardent tenors, devout
altos, and that ecstatic soprano
shimmer like sun on the sea below—

odd that it's constant racket serves
to channel such choirs. To believe
these harmonies are harvested through

two wind-sucking thrusters hurtling
this tube toward Europe, I concede,
proves I'm a bit psychotic. I do

hear the chorale, and have by the creek
where a cascade, white water, white noise,
drew me back on my walks as a kid.

In the dorm the heat's humming pipes,
in Harvard Square the din where I hawked
the weekly *Phoenix* to make a few bucks,

on the bus between Boston and Philly....
And, as the hiss-and-ring of my tinnitus
takes more share of my auditory

acuity, I have less need to fly
like this between Reykjavik and Glasgow
to listen to the singing invisible

company in the tiers rising,
who knows, far as the stars. So it seems
to a mad guy, angels between his ears.

Note

Told I'd see Mars if I looked.
Remembered to look as I turned
south down 30th for the house.

And there in the east, not far
west of the just-past-full moon,
brighter, steadier than a star,

wearing his blood-in-the-river
tinge, I was sure, there he was—
that warrior, salute him or not.

Before Going In

These old cement steps, chipped,
patched, thin chunks cracked loose
again—must be the years of rain
come out of the west. Back

from a long summer day trapped
at close indoor work, halfway
up to the porch I turn, sit down,
and rest my eyes on the gold-green

distances in that gap between houses
across the street. That edge of the seen
world goes coppery by the minute.
The trees breathe and speak. Another

aloneness is inside the house. One says
my home. Isn't *home* in the ancient sense
ours? Two robins cross north,
a loose tandem over the treetops—

low sun flashes a breast blood-orange.
I'm impressed by the worm-catchers'
deftness in air—at home in it, each
wingbeat a fresh pulse into the as-yet

unseen. And all the leaves in unison
thought on a gust—each leaf
stemmed to the rest, the roots, at home
in their helplessness. It's my guess

I'm the exile here, on my own
steps. I'll lock myself in
for the night, safe as a man can be
on this earth. And under the sheets

I'll travel, waking with little
grasp of where I'll have been. For now,
out here, the soft-lit world is solitude's
nest, my perch the planet turning,

surface a thousand miles an hour
east as I watch the sun submerge.
Yes, some of my nature stretches
across and under the streets and lots,

prairies, malls, stadiums, lakes
and seas and cemeteries, to touch
the molecular shreds of any
who've never been sure they were home.

There's the first star, high to the south.
I suspect it's no star but Jupiter,
not twinkling, just wobbled a bit
in this atmosphere. Dispersed

particulates further scatter the sunset
red to a stir, a glow, while the air allows
bluer light to speed on overhead
toward forever. Here, in this private

betweenness, back from the day's facts
and not yet behind my door, I can feel it—
the air riddled with ancestral flecks,
the char of old cook-pots and bones,

specks of blood, tiny polymer
snippets of eyelash and nail, the dust
left of wanderers' lips, afloat
in the mix of all pasts. Through the dim

a kid on his bike glides the sidewalk,
and I imagine his atoms dancing
with mine in a flyway of Canada geese
up the Inside Passage over the endless

slopes of evergreens. Home is a heartbeat,
a tent flap lifted on breath. Or it's all this
orbit and flight, future and lost,
feather, thought, and aloneness.

Goodnight Rhyme

The night is like others—two primal
carnivores under the covers, arms out
in mutual cuddle, clock set—civil

and absent apparent unrest. But look out—
this, love's bed, is a valley of red
sloughs and marshes, silted with doubt

and old hurt, and till one of us is dead
or longer, we're wound up like two
caduceus serpents head-to-head,

a symmetry of the undoing we'll do
to each other. Love is our sunder
of hide, a tear through the tissue

down to where name is no matter, under
the grudge oaths and prayers engraved
in our scrimshaw of bone—love, our thunder

up from inside to rupture the staves,
to let pour the flood out of the core,
out through the vortex of hisses and raves

where we're molten, molted and no more
known to ourselves or each other—marrow
and crave, we are door after door

down uncounted caverns all sorrows
dark veins and burning lakes, no final
floor or far shore, and no tomorrow.

Time

Eternity is in love with the
productions of time.

—William Blake,
The Marriage of
Heaven and Hell

So We Spoke

Can't wait, we heard our self say,
as we sped through the gray whatever
terrain (we forget, though I bet
it was grainy)

              toward the animate
moment, checking again again
its ordinate and abscissa. Was it
a restaurant, a bed, a precipice,
place meant to wake us?

                  Somewhere
in front of us, didn't the present await?
Already its live dyes bled
through the windshield and our eyes
to bathe our amygdalae (they writhe
as I speak of it now),

               as we headed
across the state line into blossom
land, where the road's dashes end
at the edge of the plain.

            We knew
it was there, our fest, our communion,
our two hemispheres at last enmeshed,
each word a splash of new color, each number
a cascade of notes (I saw in the air
a clarinet, flute, guitar…).

           And before
we could open our ventricles to it, there
it was, a flickering tunnel through

the jeweled foliage of wonder, a blinking
among the stars, an aortic shiver
(it must've involved some kind of chemo-
electric charge),

              and as we emerged
we saw it diminish into the blurred
geometry swallowed in our side mirrors.
So we spoke to our self again,
of that exquisite and mysterious
instant. *Wasn't it…. Wasn't it….*

Not White

White dogwood in bloom, faint-veined
leaf-petal quartets like fine cotton
fountained out on their stemlets

into the June sun, pointing
everywhere in the most unassuming
enticement to pollen-bearers, these

bright pennons don't have to spell it
out, I'm not white and was never
so innocent. Here, under this

dear dogwood, I'm a shade
in the range of earths, bruise-stained
and tinted hints of the breathless

blood in my veins. Never the white
skin on the warming milk before
the stir of my mother's wooden spoon.

Never like starlight, never
the white of the moon. Here under
the hung tiers of the dogwood's gown,

in the dark of my involuted gray
matter, my thought-mutters wait
for the first curled tips to tinge brown.

This Disappearing

Into what is to come, foot down
on the pedal, up the serpentine grade
past all the tall blond grass, as if

on a long ramp, I'm taking off,
pale purple space at the crest. What
next? Do I divine it? Sky says

I won't fly far. Maybe a bite
in that cowtown ahead. A room
for the night? Radio goes to static

just as the car hurtles over the top,
the tires do lift off like I'd thought,
at least a first inch off the planet

till the world grabs us back, flesh
and metal to the macadam, rocketeer
wish lost and I'm here in this

drier expanse, sunset-rusted
dust, vast lace of stemmy brush. How far
in front of us is it there's no hint out of

the imminent? A hawk, yards up
in the dusk glow—dark bullet's wings
beating the air back, speeding

fast as my whirring descent—pitches
in an unforeseeable instant
down out of sight, too quick

for even the atmosphere under
its wings to have sensed it, an act
no presence could have announced

till after the fact. I imagine
the mouse, or is it lizard? The hawk's
attack is possessed of a portent

the prey's atoms could shiver with, if
for a breath till the talons impinge.
The slopes ahead lavender drifts,

and I haven't the wish, this moment,
for a clue out of the great suspense.
For now I'll cherish the hapless

careen. Car caresses the curve
come alongside a low river tinted
silver amid its stones. In this

disappearing light, the valley's riddled
with unknowable gasps and trickles,
the river a molted snake hide.

Yahrzeit

In this instance, it's early May.
I've taken note, the moon is near
full. Here where I live,

not where he remained and entered
the earth, there are salmonberries
already plumped and reddened. Here,

far from the house I left and the year
he last hung his wooden Wilson racquet
up on its hook in that clean garage,

I've seen him scuffing up close
to the net, heard his forehand grunt,
nearly touched the sweat on his brow

as I did when he thrashed on his final
bed. Here, I've seen a barred owl
shadowing on a low cedar bough.

These days rainless and open, vision
permitted between here and above.
And of the wind, it isn't much

more than a few gusts sweeping through
from the shore around dusk. It scatters
petals torn from the cherry and plum

as I walk toward home. I've thought
I might light a candle, or write a poem.
Both wouldn't hurt. Now while I can,

while the earth's in just the position
it was, regarding the sun, as when
he left. Three years it's been,

and, although I'm not much
taken up with tradition, as he wasn't
one to ever speak of the oneness

of all there is, let the candle be lit.
Some of him must've entered the light.
What I see by it, let my hand write.

After Parking at Starbucks

I've opened the door to her dark
seat in the car. Mom offers
a skeletal arm, skin loose around
bone and what thready muscle
remains under blue tortuous veins.

I bow and take hold with one hand
a cradle for the creak of her elbow,
one where stiffened fingers can rest.
My hesitation's hidden as I am
its lone witness—something fine

and brittle might break as I lift it
away from its place, like that china
cup I fumbled and dropped soon
as I'd slid it off of the hutch
for a better look one morning

when I was five or six. It had been
her mother's, I heard her sharpened
voice insist as we stared
at the scatter of jagged white bits
on the floor's innocent oak. It was

what remained of a set—one cup-
ful of distant comfort. Had I been
more careful…. Gently I tug on her
arm, help her stand, and steady her
imperceptibly as she shuffles

beside me. The old shatters keep us
company—a chattering wake.
There's never a lack of the broken—
I hear a muffled clatter, a girl
in pieces it isn't too late to hold.

Two Men Saying Goodbye

It was clear, he was down to days.
My printed boarding pass declared
US Airways Terminal B
next morning. Should I leave,

I'd miss his eyelids parting less
and less, the gaps between gasps
lengthening, and the last reflex
kiss at the Diet Pepsi's straw.

As he blinked at me, I believed
he saw someone he loved. I wouldn't go
so far as to say son or father,
but a glow of his own life in me.

My brother would stay. Oh, he'd have to
sleep at his condo, deal with a few things
early each day, but he'd be back
on hand at the bedside rail. He'd hold

the old man's head up to help him
sip the cold from the can
while the fever of brain-swell rose
till the burgeoned gel pressed the breath drive

closed. My brother would stand there
while Mom sat by the window and dozed.
I'd fly back to my coast, while Dad lost
the last shred of sense. I intoned

Shalom Aleichem to him as I turned—
"Peace be upon you," as it was offered
in doorways and on the streets where he was
a boy. Eyes widened, he called out

that ancient goodbye we'd never said
to one another. Who were we then?
My shoes struck loud on hard floor
down the hall past all those rooms.

Shadow-Ink

You did hold me. It happened
days ago, your arms real
as these arms I wrapped around you,

and on this bed, where the light's been
kept to a trickle by the curtains
I hung for our aloneness of two.

It's quiet as well, which helps
memory fill its several dimensions—
again your scent, intricate

blend of breath and essences,
and your taste, the dissolved
salts of your skin, and the sweat-oiled

friction between our surfaces, and
the vision, smooth plenitude wet
with a splash of predawn lumens.

I keep it this dark and this close
to silence, so I can imagine,
with little distraction, what was,

even from some dreamy perches
alongside where we lay, or suspended
just under the ceiling, or peeking

from outside through the gap
between fabric and sill, to see
the two thrilled glistening people

we were, a morning that might've been
eons ago or a figment. I wish it were
now. How else to be sure?

I want memory to be sufficient.
Its witnesses are with me—sworn
company of the senses. I have

selected a jury. Favorable
angels hover at various angles
to assess recollection's evidence.

Yes, lying here at the scene,
I can decide you've loved me.
It's like seeing it written

with a twig in sand, a breath
before a tide fan sweeps it
away, the shadow-ink spread

in one swipe from the record. When
is it ever enough, to think
of the past? In its absence

doubt is a fast-risen sea—
I am about to inhale it.
Come back. Come hold me.

Seasonal

The bees made their way in again. I saw
the restrained cringes and winces we each
couldn't help, as they hummed poking
the air like aimless silhouette bullets
between us and the bright windows. It looked
like that year they crawled through the gap
where the hearth stones didn't quite meet cedar
siding or plaster. The kids were young then
and I hated to see them scared. This time
it meant something different. I can't say what,
but I didn't call the man
who knew what to do. Summer would end,
and the bees would be swept away too.

Birds Over a Marsh

Like most, I quit my babbling
quick—the oral machinery worked
the local syllabic tricks. Lips

permitted *puppet* and *ball*. It took
the tongue for *love* and *drink*. I sprouted
teeth and could *think*. Made for this

aren't we? So I can *tell* you
my sight. Those small black birds,
scarlet bands on their wings—those

the males, of a few who've stayed
though the sun called them south—surveille
from the taller cattails and twigs

surrounding the pond. They traverse it
in forays, for the hatch of tiny bugs
risen this first warm late-winter day.

I have the words. So why is it
these last years I'm again mouthing
nonsense? I stand here on mud

to spy out over a baffle of reeds,
and spout a lilting scat to capture
those dashing dark holdouts' dips

and rises. In my undiscovered language
I say they're bold, praise how they sport
those yellow-fringed blaze-red epaulets

over the cold pool below. I call them
forgettable things, for no one to know.
But approach unnoticed, and you'll catch

my gibberish, close, I suppose, to Yiddish,
much like the noise of the air I inhaled
while I still crawled. Right off

my errant tongue, through lips
relieved of their civic duty, tumbles
this mix of sonorants and obstruents,

inflected as might be a very small
child's, prattle meant for no ears
but my own. Though in it at times

I hear the old ironical plaints,
the immigrants' worried wishes, late-night
solicitudes to a chill-wakened toddler

in my grandmother's arms—such feeling,
but without the *about*. Is this now
my report of an ornithological sighting,

or do I mourn the migration of young
who tromped this thicketed wetland with me
to christen these *prince birds*? It could be

both, and more, this heart's broadcast
crossing all distance and death, no matter
the others' awareness. Or do I mutter

what somebody might've said descending
the tower God didn't want built? Maybe
I've salvaged this early music to manage

spouseless after so long in the household
hubbub of marriage. Or have I gone
back at last for the mumbling creature

I left in my urge to belong? I keep up
a burbling, like a stream—sounds
like it trickles over its cow-licked stones

along the edge of a field, somewhere near
the Vilna. The song will not leave me
alone. Someone young has moved in-

to the bone hut again, now
that the broken-glass promise is broken,
all the kids flown, the old gone

earthen—I come to wander
this windblown home, to savor
the unnamable swoops of wonder.

The Impossible

Early May, a cool evening, late
enough in this life I welcome the stray
cottonwood tuft on my jacket sleeve,

loose tangle of fine white hairs
caught on the nap of the light
wool weave. I watch it shiver

there in an imperceptible breeze,
thin airy bundle, sunset-tinted,
stuck for the moment inches

up from my cuff. No bother,
no omen, it doesn't suggest
the least imminence. It's meant

for me as much as the white strip
I'd slip from a crisp fortune cookie.
It hasn't been sent nor found me

an essential stop on its way
to fulfill its fertility, this
weightless fluff seed raft—no news

out of the unseen in its touching
down, nor in how it takes off
just now on a faint gust, gliding

out over the asphalt of 65th
with no eye for the soil, no small wheel
nor rudder, adrift as its countless

blind cousins the snow of the *Populus*
trees clustered a block or so south
by the footbridge above the ravine.

No steerage but wind for the gene-bearing
husks, most never to open
their cores to moist earth, they'll dissolve

back into the world in doorways, gutters,
cracks in the road and sidewalk, stuck
returning to dust with no chance

to unfold. Some have the luck
to settle on spring-wet dirt, uncoil
their code scrolls, sprout, and spread out

their deltoid leaves, to become
the cottonwood trees, shedding their own
bright cotton. By no prophecy,

no keen discernment nor any
deserving, another spring evening,
I was a kite of loose fiber let go

on buffeting currents and scudded
to a weedy loam patch. I took,
and my heart hatched in the ground of this

fortunate madness, love. Here I am
in its deepening shade, where I claim
the impossible—that this will last

longer than the broad cottonwoods stand
in their seasoned slow slow dance.
And all by the catch of a thread.

The Temperature

My grandfather would loosen his tie
then his collar, fingers in to the side,
a tug or two, a harsh whisper

phew and a grumble *hot in here*, even
when it was brisk by the window.
He'd open it more, and we'd hear

my grandmother's over-the-shoulder plea
from where she leaned at the sink
or at the oven checking the chicken,

such a chill you're letting in.
Each had an embodied opinion.
But it was never the temperature.

Two in one life, same bed all the nights
a tent of communion of scents, confusion
of twin breath-hollows, memories

braided into a confluence, and the one
emptiness blown in under the sash
all there is to fill in the absence

where the kids were—how can we live
like this and keep our hearts wrapped
in our separate skins? How do we not

collapse into a plasm, a blur?
They yelled at each other. Maybe that
helped—provided a chasm.

He huffed and couldn't sit still.
She stood and cooked. Did they ever
kiss? The window skirmish went on

till he was lowered. Then she'd sit down
at the kitchen table in the cool air
she'd let waft in, and wait for him.

My Brother's Own Throat

Two near-invisible old guys edging
the surf, we amble north, keeping
the constant Atlantic's loud whisper off
to our right with its ledge the horizon.

And to our left, the slow single-file
procession of tall hotels seems endless
as well. We shamble on through
squads of next-to-naked small kids

splashing the shallows. We're in
our clothes. My brother jigs clear
of each frothy fan and keeps dry. I've got
my cloth slip-ons and pant legs soaked.

Gulls, terns, and sandpipers congregate
close, mingled like gangs gotten used
to each other. Human twosomes saunter
beside us in swimsuits. They appear

comfortable so exposed. Their talk
drowns fast in the jostled air.
My brother sputters into the drone
how the last romance spun down

and crashed—around him, the laughter
of churned water, of children
and birds, and of the chugging
single-prop up there lugging its banner

for a new lotion across the blue span.
And out of my brother's own throat
a guttering tone—he savors the joke,
as if it's on some other old man.

Love Poem Written in Broad Darkness

I've been advised not to say moon,
not to say heart too often, watch out
for uses of black, deep, or sea,
and never say soul. Don't call the sky
heavens, avoid vast and infinite,
do not apply spirit, don't toss around
love, and leave the flowers out of it.

Desire's a risk, hope hazardous,
and longing best called something else.

So I'm well-warned, no swooner
staring up at that white boat riding
the night. It bears no letter,
no trinket, no tincture sent
to pleasantly jigger my ticker. And no
far shore across that immense water,

no port with a tower tuned
to any of our dazed whimpers.
Our infrared affections unfold
like idiot blooms on loose bony stems
till we end. Our breath leaves no evidence,
no echo off that great body of nothing
but distance. Still, I could call the heights
bruise-blue and you might feel a little
impact, or say I see coal-shine
embedding those promising sparks.

I will say street, as I'm on it.
Shouldn't say solitude but I will,
less alone than minutes ago
in the jostle and slosh of the pub. This

moment I've saved to say love
just once more in this poem, your face
some literal elsewhere, close as ever.

I drift under the halide glare
and, like a fallen dogwood tetrad
crinkled, discolored, missed by the rake,
I scrape along the curb in the draft
of a passing car. Scent of match sulfur
or gunpowder, smell of fatal mistake

in this shaken air, I'm a late idiom
out of place. I'll aim and fire
my antique flare like a brief near star
in your dream-sky. I'll call it a sign.

You'd say it's not there. I'll say my soul did
what it could while there was time.

Here After

Dying elsewhere is sudden, out
in the sun—dying here a white curtain,
nurse when you press the right button.

Elsewhere is an outdoor market
stun-blossom, blood flesh and flatbread
charred and shredded, a bone ash spread.

Here is a quiet long shock, dumb winter
windows' stare at the pallid potatoes
and sliced bird on your plastic platter.

The dying here and the dying there—
you're born to one matter or
the other. Chaos will come

as magnificently symmetrical viral
particles, or circulating free radicals
prodding your chromosomes to double

and double like burgeoning insurgents' camps, or
surgical mishaps, impromptu blasts...
and slow or fast, thereafter

the dying lasts. What will be
the echo won't be explosion or scream
or siren, nor the beeping of cardiac

monitor till it goes monotone, nor
the low lone whimper of someone
you've left here after, but this

resonance: Once, when you were
intact, as the machines wheeled past,
the smears being mopped up and all

the gathered dispersed, you'd taken
someone fresh-numb with loss in your arms,
and later, she held another.

The Rose

The late sidelong light's red-gold
on the walls, on the tall dry grass,

on the moon's face low and immense
across the expanse, in the distant

sky trapped in that fire-lit shallow
creek, its mirrored streaks of cloud...

not many breaths of this, not many
heartbeats, and what will keep

in memory still less, so it seems,
so it is, that between pulses,

between blinks, perception's presence
opens, as if it knows, and lets

in as through parted lips the instant's
sweet and coppery tincture. Even

though it is brief as the moment before
getting back in the car for the droning

hours over the mountains, even
though it is years you might bear

your marrow under the stars, now
you've tasted the light of the flower,

the rose whose petals, you know,
you and all these things are.

Song Toward Dawn

Same dark, eyes open as closed.
So I can watch the old wonders
recast. New sets. New clothes.

No wind, no branches scratching
the walls, furnace dormant for summer,
it's easy as ever to hear,

to the brush-beat of the carotids,
the repeated curses and plaints—
declarations I'd never make,

but there's no one else present,
is there? All my years gathered,
a gifted ensemble, faces

amalgams of firsts and lasts,
a lover with the eyes of my mother,
an early Aunt Dorothy in a clay mask,

barista wearing the smile of the dead
grandfather I was named after, brother
wrinkled with Baltic rivers.

And the old woman my daughter,
heart's halves in her hands,
still dazed by the home wars.

This is the stage. Michelle shows me
hers in the bushes, we're five,
and she's the ageless angel

who arrives in the dream garden I find,
she places her palm on my belly
and I hear the storm I am in my core....

My father, white-shirted glad gladiator
whistling at the wheel of his black Buick,
leans back, become an ancient

Passover celebrant, tumor'd and pale
in his hospice bed, and cries
for the hallucinated hot soup

he knows his mother's prepared
for us all in the nonexistent
kitchen. And there's the kitchen,

to the left, in an evening light
through tall windows that open
onto the heights. And the land lit

soft like a worn cloth, calls
for a song, notes of smoke you can't see
in the dark, and won't by the dawn.

Union

*...space by itself, and time
by itself, are doomed to fade
away into mere shadows, and
only a kind of union of the two
will preserve an independent
reality...*

—Hermann Minkowski
(Einstein's college
mathematics teacher),
1908

Geometry of the Orbits

Did we speed up the stars?
Night's over, you've risen—what
can I savor? Those high notes

the birds utter usher a close.
And the crocuses, already gone—
have I shown you one? One

dawn will be the last. The catch
in my throat, a choke on the wind.
We're at the prow of a fast boat.

Or the heart's own sharp minute
hand's clicked past, nicking
the larynx—a little clock joke.

I did kiss the back of your neck.
Its arc belongs to the long
geometry of the orbits—there,

the endlessness. And we are
permitted peeks into the black
behind each other's irises.

Pull of the Moon

I paddled where currents converged
from the sides of a narrow island.

The tide, coursing hard, rejoined
itself in a churn south of the spit

formed, I guessed, by centuries
of just such motion. Hordes of froth

collided. Schools of bright herring boiled
the surface—a mob of gulls bobbed,

hovered, dove, and stuffed their gullets
on those silvery swarms. The sizzle

drew in a few gleaming salmonid nomads
breaching ecstatic.... I was lost

in the thrall. There'd be no paddling
back to the beach till the slack,

so I drifted and turned like a twig
of cliff-side madrona blown from a shore,

tossed and soaked but safe enough
in the troughs of the chop. I remember

this when I think of us, what we call
our attraction—pull of the moon

on the one sea, its reunion, once
the land's no longer between us.

Mouth

Little sucker—his mother's nipple
mechanism's jinxed by his thirst.

There is too much need in this house—
she feels eaten. And that old

louse who seeded her, he's out again
late reportedly pleasing the boss

who's got a divorce to talk about. What if
all this life's an insatiable mouth?

she wonders, resting her forehead
against the cold glass of the world

in the bathroom mirror. Little *pisher*—
this ma-ma won't take the call,

cannot let it drag her down
the hall to the railed bed and the piercing

squeal that already explodes in her head.
What if the whole world is one hollow

appeal to be fed? Every one of us
not yet a toddler—pope and president,

every last UN ambassador—it makes her
wish her eyes could exude a few tears,

but bitterness clogs the ducts. Unfortunate
fusser, he knows without thought

he's the big trouble. He'll take a bottle
and she'll go to the kitchen for hers.

Little cur—he'll syphon the most vital
part of her life, his bestial bite

right out of the middle. It will not be
a pleasure. She feels his wail—

the diapered commander has her
hard by her cardiac muscle in his

telekinetic grip, as if
he were still in her, digging

his digits up through her diaphragm
into her left ventricle. Could it be

self after self—one swum out
of the other since conception's own birth,

all from the same subspace lagoon—
tunnels a lineage of the original

urge, and we are the sucking
tubes poking the future, strung out

as long as the sun heats the pool, each of us
hung out to die, a wish out of water?

she muses, eye-to-eye with her silvery
immaterial double. She listens—

a gasp and sigh, a glottal gurgle,
soft exhausted moan of why-bother

out of her caged little *wild animal*,
a surrender, after all, to her

refusal to arrive. Relief
and shame will sink down and dissolve

inside like the droplets of angostura
she'll add to her rye to call it

a cocktail. And she'll drink
to her child, who, when she peeks—

tiny pucker of lips a sign
he dreams he's the fishlike creature

he is in the world's first waters—seems
like a needless angel.

I'll See Her Turning

If she wasn't asleep, she wasn't still.
What a little girl had learned
of eternal urgency in an immigrant
home burned in her body.

Survival was busy—the dishes,
the laundry, the lengthening
list of what we're out of already,
the baby to lift from the crib—

she'd say *There's never enough
time.* And too many tasks—
didn't the walls insist on the prints
she found? The craft of the frames

no less a necessity. Saving
the gift wrap from this holiday
till the next; composing her own
earrings, bracelets, and necklaces

out of the scraps of consignments
left in glass cases in dusty shops;
sewing on salvaged brass buttons
to enliven drab coats—such missions

her most familiar comfort.
Lithuania held the Vilna again
as her hands rescued and fried
the livers of chickens she'd roast.

There were years of leftovers
foiled with care, labeled in bold
magic marker, tucked in the freezer
for a scarcity her bones remembered.

And she could dance, into the moment
free of the past—no mop
nor sink to lean at nor toddler's cry,
an effortless loft. I'll recall that,

assured of her joy. She could float
outside the rush of time, above
all that was called-for. I'll see her
turning, out on the floor of the sky.

Signature

At birth, what was I, some
fourteen-billion-year-old dust
clustered as a limbed self-
driven fusser? Repurposed

fusion stuff, thrust
from countless novae, my atomic
populace had seen the hottest
hell all time could throw us.

Then cooled, composed, a creature—
like a snowdrift risen just
where temperature and wind conspire,
mist gone crystalline

and there's a contour, spine
a little serpentine. It shifts
by grainy increments, appears
to sidewind, to desire,

till it's washed away by just what
forces shape it. I melt
by my own metabolic fire,
if nothing else. This self,

what is it? By the next
warm day, it isn't. I've watched
my father thrash and lose his words,
unknow himself and me,

a self-erasing signature,
blown wisp of star-spray. He
looked out with pure first wonder.
At death, how new I'll be.

Catch

All the fathers are gone, under
the grass, above us in the earth's
greenhouse haze, in stream silts
where the burial hills are awash
in the unprecedented monsoons,

some never found, swamped shot
in the rice marshes and ultimately
part of the crop, some taken in bits
as they sank into the mouths of fish
and bottom scavengers, some chopped

into manageable chunks and wrapped
to be kept from the air and stashed
behind Sheetrock while the cops passed
for unbroadcast reasons—all
the fathers, it sometimes seems, are gone,

while it's only mine and maybe a billion
or two others, while in the park
by the lot for the market one squats
to get eye-level with his wide-eyed son
to steady the small heart's tremble. Not all

the fathers are gone. All *I* remember
from when I was little, the laughers
and smokers and golfers and TV repairmen,
who might, any one of them, once
in a summer, before supper, come out

on the street to toss us the ball for a bit
to get us to discover that supple
give in the hand that can take

more of the world in its grasp—all
those old men are lost. So it's hard

to believe what I see—a man
in a white shirt, sleeves to the elbows, holding
a pink rubber ball in one hand to give it
that easy up-and-down hefting as if
to assess its weight which is so slight,

inches from his enthralled son's face,
before handing it over to see
if the boy who must only be three can cock
his arm back next to his head and hurl
that microcosmic planet aloft

on its next heavenly arc. It is all
my fathers dissolved in the past.
Here's a dad, yet to be sloughed
or sequestered, to leave this eye-to-eye
moment to be remembered. This

crouching pop and his pal, could be
on the grass outside my earliest house—
oh the phones and cars were different,
we had other names for the wars
we watched on our monitors, but it was

a facile animal of the same lot,
bent low to show me, out
in the solar glare, how to plot
the curve of the world, before
he rose, and was no longer there.

In the Shade by the Water
—for my daughter

Our sorrows meet in one shadow, one
stream, like the ravine creek we'd follow
when you were small. I'm back

there in my daydream, your hand in mine
under the tall summer trees, still cool
midday on the path along our little river,

you crouch over slugs, stroke the moss
coats on the earth and alder trunks, talk
silk architecture among the spiders,

squawk with the crows as they laugh
at their own jokes. Eternally cool here
below the sun-cooked bungalows.

Home we'd walk from, it's no more.
I left you, let the screen door swat
the jamb as I strode off alone, years before

you could leave too. Left you in that quiet
cavern, floor bared of my Persian rugs,
fridge groaning its hunger from inside

the kitchen. Over the spent wine bottles,
fruit flies in clouds like ghosts of roses
I'd brought you and Mom. Your welcome

to a new loneliness. I wouldn't let myself
see it then. Now you're across town,
a run-down shared rental, more life in it,

more laughter. You've had me there
once. Here, in the shade by the water
where both our sorrows flow, you step

out of your shoes, as you would, to wade.
I still don't know how to atone.
Your feet slip into the cold on the stones.

I Know You from Somewhere

For every atom belonging to me as good belongs to you.
—Whitman

His sun-toughened ruddiness stands out
in the spring shade as his face enlarges
before a dim backdrop of the trees' quiet
columned arcade. His dust-wake shows
as he shuffles through a few beams. Hunched
in a blue parka I'd bet is his bedroll,

he's close enough now I can smell
his private atmosphere of tobacco,
seasoned sweat, tooth rot and rotgut and
I don't know, mold of wet foam cushion
pressed into service beneath him on the dirt
not far in this park. He's stopped

on the path in front of me, swollen hands
hanging purple and busy with tremor,
hair a dark mat like tide-river weed
where the ebb's left it flat in the night,
cracked lips undulant like the worms
Haldol brings with it, eyes

double-glazed under smudged hefty lenses
and froth-white cataract clouds. Out
through the yellow-browned gate of his teeth,
his thick tongue squeezes a crowd
of sounds, a spittled and rasped
Know where the Safeway is?

I envision a few crumpled one-dollar
bills and a ballast of quarters waiting
to spill from his pockets, on the counter
a bottle of golden toxin. I picture

the nip and the guzzle out through the nozzle
noosed in brown paper, and the doze

back in his leaf-mulch-carpeted cove.
I see him blinking up at the sparkling
canopy. He is eased, and knows
he swims Earth's night-and-day helix home.
I can't think where the Safeway is,
not while I look into this holographic

mirror, this him, this other self's
face I wish to disown, to make his
alone. For which it's too late—by now
we're woven into entanglement, even
though we remain unnamed to each other
and curtains of haze lie between us.

This is the braiding of fate. In the shimmer
the wind-shaken leaves make, stranger
to stranger, though we're each veiled
in the murk of our sloughed thought-scales,
our looking takes us a moment
upriver, into the spawn beds of suns,

spore-mist before all the divisions,
where we float till we're each born
to one street or father or war or another,
and where we must still hover after
the pulsing's done. I don't recall
where the Safeway is till I've veered off,

sidestepped around him, and the daze lifts.
The market's a half-mile past the park
the way he's already drifting. He calls
from behind, *I know you from somewhere.*

I don't turn my head, but mutter *True*,
as if, through the star-water, he'll hear.

Love's Home

The body emits. I remember
my mother gathering up the sheets
as I stood by the bed, convinced

I was worse than useless. She hid
her grimace as best she could. Then
there was blood, red ooze at the knee

as I'd done it again, careless, her wince
as she daubed it, cotton wet with Bactine…

and the cries, so often
storming up from the lungs
to force open the grit-gate of teeth….

It's impossible not to emit,
not to press love to its tolerance
limit. How is it

I checked my gag each time as I mopped
my sick kid's chin and chest
again with the rinsed rag?

And wasn't there the elder who fell
as he sat where you'd removed the chair?
Scalp a shell cracked on the floor,

it dripped. You fled—didn't help.
And hadn't a matchbook flared
in the old man's palm, that weeping

crater in flesh a terror, a wish
he'd never touch you with that hand again?

Haven't we each more than once failed
love's test? And as I get old,
I'll emit more, not less—

the whimpers and fluids and breaths
we've dreamed we controlled while it was
chaos taking its time with us—

till it exceeds your threshold, I can't
wash or shower or wipe fresh
any part of myself enough, and you,

young lover, will have had enough,
like my mother, her hour

every two days or so in the chair
in the far corner of my father's last room,

the tumor inside his skull insisting
his body emit every last thing.

Or is there a turn? If you fall
first, is it in me to change
the soaked surgical dressing? Or you might

learn, by love's stubborn duration
alone, this concoction of scents,
this collage of the unhealable

wounds and their seepages, must prove
at last endurable. This is love's home.

All Your Ages

Years furrowed and slacked your skin,
wrote new lines of silent narrative
round your eyes and lips, tinged
your teeth with tides of tea and wine,
thinned your arms, drew your breasts down,
blew sand through your soft voice,

and I was surprised—I saw the timeless
you, who wore the creaseless cheek
I'd stroked the first morning we woke
in the world together. I had the scent
of your early sweat to remember,
to blend with the further fermented.

What sun and oxygen did to your hair,
bleached gray as the Cape's beach houses
we passed on our honeymoon bikes, I took
as no more real than the walnut sheen
I could still see. My heart doctored
the present's parchment, inked in scenes

from as far as some of your childhood
snapshots. I dared such composites.
I was another of love's collagists,
had your full breasts in my hands
in the inescapable blur of touch-sense
and memory. My desire rose

and rose in a blossoming wonder
with all your ages. But I watched you close
your scrapbook on me. Was it your father
backhanding your mother once more
when I'd raise a palm to the sky? I see
in my heart's eye a gasping wide-eyed girl.

Night on the Way Back from the Metolius River

We talked out our blues to the dark,
backs to a log, seated on dirt
the summer'd dried out. Before us
the trees like silhouette curtains parted—
the starry backdrop went back
and back, a oneness of distance

and time, what had cast us all out
on our world lines. We had parked
our families in the motel by the road,
glad for a walk out into the dusk,
chance for a smoke, maybe a tavern's red
sign-glow among the conifer trunks

as we scuffed gravel shoulder around
the long bend. There was no tavern,
but a dirt road to a small lot, someone's
not-yet cabin, and without discussion
we'd sat down for the show. Night,
what can it know? For all the time

it held in its view, it told us nothing—
not how in years we'd be out of our houses,
out of the blame showers, immersed
in the lulls and surges of uncertain touch,
wanderers like when we were young
but old. Could the night have said

there's another road, shown the invisible
need in love's angry bed, turned us
toward not away? I wonder—with all

the star-theater's space before us, for all
our talk of our thwarted urges—what
if the dark spoke we'd have heard.

Temple of Late Snow

Wind from the north brought the cold back
over the crocuses and purple hellebore.

Brought down a late trace of snow, laced
a row of tall cedars I strode under,

and I saw there the elders' fringed shawls
embroidered with prayer, remembered

those beards murmuring over a scroll
in a lost world's code. I'd not understood,

but saw fires and swords in a brightness
that never lit streets in my neighborhood.

I've walked to the shore to watch the wind
write its white lines. A lone cormorant

beats black wings low over the unreadable
water, the bird's chant fast and silent.

No Other

I could be the one you'd choose
to cry to. Well, not choose—

you'd come tripping out of the crowd,
tossed, extruded. No, not crowd—

what you'd've thrashed through to shore
to not drown. No shore

you'd aim for, but at last some ground
to collapse to. Not your ground

nor mine, though it'd welcome the roots
you'd dragged this far. If not roots,

what are these thirsty fibers that matter
more to us than our hearts? No matter

that we'd be lost, displaced as ever,
despite the maps the locals offer, not ever

quite suggesting we stay, their smiles
well meant, though they're not smiles—

you could let me be the one other
you trust, as no other

wanderer will be here to welcome you
out of the fog. Not welcome you

so much as go to my knees to see you
trudging my way. I wouldn't see you

as one more mirror. Such use,
I'd know, would be no use.

Here He Is

Six years ago today, a man I called
Dad slipped from his robe of skin,

left it behind in that hospital bed
where I'd visited. He set out early

that morning, first of May, days
after I'd seen the hawk perched high

on that gold ball top of the flagpole
over the building he drifted in. I'd gone

out to walk along Darby Creek,
to remember and think, and saw the hawk

lift off on its wide wings. Six years
and his presence strong, I don't call him

Dad so much. My hair gray as his turned
after the rounds of aimed radiation,

and by my living room chair, there he is
nine or ten smiling out of a frame,

and this morning out back of the kitchen,
the forsythia's blossomed, sprigs

bowing in wind as they had in the yard
when I was a kid, and Dad on his way

down the stairs to work would wave. Then,
he was tens of years younger than I am

now—I think of him
not so much as father, but someone

I love in my lineage. Here he is,
wings' shadow quick over yellow blooms.

What I Did

My hope's a child's. My grandmother
stood over the sink in the summer
morning's south window glow, holding
the rounded box of frozen strawberries
under the faucet's warm rush, her voice
a murmur of pleasure, till she was sure
the insides were thawed enough. Soon,
she'd set the white bowl on the yellow
Formica table, the deep red fruit cold,
sliced, ready to lift in the big spoon
from the pool of sweet juice.

                This is one
scrap, an age-browned crayoned sheet
tucked in among others—stick-figure
fathers and silvery terriers, thick-outlined
houses, chimneys uncoiling black springs,
smudged tulips, fangs of white fence—
such pages, stuffed in a secret hurry
into the slots between a kid's ribs,
hold up only so well as they're slid
free by these wrinkled hands. See
what I did? Stored the light that poured in
over the rooftops across the alley,
over my grandpop's tomato vines,
in through the kitchen window and lit
my grandmother's cheeks and lips.

                    Creased
documents coming apart as they open
to my stiff fingers, still, I can taste
the strawberries' smooth and sturdy pieces,
hear the tiny surprises of seeds'
crunch in my lost milk teeth, and savor

that rosy nectar. This creaking body's dark
shelves are crammed with a little fool's
crumbling scrolls of love's promise.
True, false—either way, this knowledge,
her soft hand leaving the bowl.

No Number of Years

I'm out in the alley, in the cold
rain with no hat on, for no reason
I know.

            And it's another
alley. I fly my sturdy red one-speed
past all possible blood spills.

                        This time
I watch from behind—there I go, smaller,
then disappear in the hedge's

                                shadow.
Rain hits my head like it will
a stone in a field.

                Warren and I
crash and our palms bleed. We press
our wounds together. Brothers we pledge.

I see him once later. Never
again. The rain's blur-shined
my lenses

            —bikes on their sides
in the laurel's shade, bent wheels
in landfill by the Delaware

                        downriver
from our streets and houses, our cries
of thrill and rage alike in the clouds,

comet-water freed from our cells
falling again in the rain
some number

                no number of years
from when.... I'll go inside
and pretend to be old again.

Sitting in a Wicker Chair in Front of a Bungalow in Seattle, Washington

I have wasted my life.
    —James Wright

Shade side of the porch post,
a lone snail climbs. It must
mourn the rain's end. The sun
warms my thighs through my pants.

The air's cool waves on my brow,
I imagine the distances
the wind's traveled to ruffle the leaves
and rock the high branches.

Slant rays through the deep red maple,
flies weaving amid the boughs
seem dazed by the beams.

A plane drones in the west.
My eyes close and open.
I'm old. I'm coming to life.

About the Author

Jed Myers grew up in Philadelphia and studied poetry
at Tufts University. While continuing to read and
write poems, he studied medicine at Case Western
Reserve and then trained in psychiatry at the University
of Washington. He settled in Seattle, where he still
maintains a private therapy practice and teaches in the
UW Department of Psychiatry.

Myers began seeking publication after the events of
September 11th, 2001. His first full-length collection,
Watching the Perseids, which chronicles his father's dying
of a glioblastoma, won the Sacramento Poetry Center
Book Award. He's authored three chapbooks, including
Dark's Channels, chosen by Tyehimba Jess for the *Iron
Horse Literary Review* Chapbook Award. Recognitions
include *Southern Indiana Review's* Mary C. Mohr Award,
the *Prime Number Magazine* Award for Poetry, *The
Southeast Review's* Gearhart Poetry Prize, *The Tishman
Review's* Edna St. Vincent Millay Poetry Prize, and, in the
UK, the McLellan Poetry Prize. Poems have appeared in
*Prairie Schooner, Rattle, Poetry Northwest, Crab Orchard
Review, The Summerset Review, Southern Poetry Review,*

Crab Creek Review, and elsewhere, including several anthologies. Two recent essays on poetry and medicine have appeared in *JAMA*. Jed Myers is Poetry Editor for the journal *Bracken*.

CPSIA information can be obtained
at www.ICGtesting.com
Printed in the USA
FFHW020236270219
50730514-56130FF